TWO
TOWNS
OVER

Also by Darren C. Demaree

A Fire Without Light (2017) — Nixes Mate Books

Many Full Hands Applauding Inelegantly (2016) — 8th House Publishing

The Nineteen Steps Between Us (2016) — After the Pause Press

Not For Art Nor Prayer (2015) — 8th House Publishing

The Pony Governor (2015) — After the Pause Press

Temporary Champions (2014) — Main Street Rag

As We Refer to Our Bodies (2013) — 8th House Publishing

TWO TOWNS OVER

Poems by Darren C. Demaree

*Winner of the 2017 Louise Bogan Award
for Artistic Merit and Excellence*

THP

Demarree, Darren C.
1st edition.

ISBN: 978-0-9965864-9-8
Library of Congress Control Number: 2017955109

Interior Layout & Cover Design by Lea C. Deschenes
Cover Photo by Michelle Frankfurter
Editing by Drew S. Cook & Tayve Neese

Printed in Tennessee, USA
Trio House Press, Inc.
Ponte Vedra Beach, FL

To contact the author, send an email to tayveneese@gmail.com.

This book is dedicated to those in Ohio and all over the world suffering from addiction to drugs or alcohol. We see you. We love you. We can and will do better to be advocates for your care.

Table of Contents

Sweet Wolf #1

We've named all of the animals
& we've put our fingers into the names
of each of them. We've dragged

their names up to our faces
& forced them to meet our made-
up world. Sometimes we are given

kisses. Sometimes there is
a great warmth. We know they
are wild. We know there is danger.

We know if we allow the sweet wolf
into our veins it will become
the alpha inside our own bodies

& yet, what a pool to drown in.
The chemicals of each breed
brings a new threat.

There have been so many Ohioans
eaten from the inside out
that I've been forced

to re-think exactly what these drugs
are in our world. They are wolves.
We've been raised by them.

SWEET WOLF #2

When we open our mouths
to resemble the beasts
you can see the color

of our saliva has changed.
We wanted a safe wreck.
We got half of that.

Now, when we howl
it's through the bubbles
that barely allow us to.

Sweet Wolf #4

The real power
is undressed
inside of us,

because that's
how actual
monsters operate.

Sweet Wolf #7

It's not life
if you're clinging
to the tall window

in your living room
because it faces
a true north.

SWEET WOLF #12

Gestures to a mask,
did you know that if you
connect the location

of every drug-house
in the Knox County area
you will see my face?

Sweet Wolf #13

Lost in the acreage,
sin can stretch out a bit,
can sing the crowd

into a burning skeleton,
can make a path
out of the ashes

of each field party
& when the sun becomes
a witness, how many

stray animals do you
think it will count?
How many sheriffs

are found sleeping
in their off-duty trucks?
It's useless to govern

most of Ohio, when most
of Ohio is smoke, is anti-
treasure, is empty alarm.

SWEET WOLF #22

Manufactured
to be
pulverized
& crystallized
& set on fire
& boiled
while the legs
are bouncing
& nobody is
going anywhere.
How much self
is left by the time
we've mastered
the science?
How much
alliance is there
between
the chemicals
& the crowd
clamoring
for them?
Isn't every hit
taken a knife
fight in an alley?
These wounds
are all
untreated;
the bodies
piling up.

Sweet Wolf #24

I thought I was a shadow.
Each needle confirmed that.
Now, I pretend to be a ghost.

SWEET WOLF #25

The home
& the temple
are quite modest

if you're passed
out on the steps
that reach them.

SWEET WOLF #29

The mother is a violet.
There never was a father.
The children are ruined

because they wanted
to choose their own
ruining. They took

a stand by lying down
& being pinned down
by engineered warmth.

Morgan Township, Ohio

All of that wallpaper
torn off into letters
& rolled into

cigarette papers
& I asked the bad goatee
about to sell me

some dream house
of methamphetamines,
why did he tear the letters

in the first place?
He said he was an artist
& he was looking

for the good glue
on the paper to help
him reach a new plane.

I didn't want the drugs.
I didn't buy the drugs.
I wanted to see Ohio

& the kind of artists
that were hiding
in the dimples

of the two-lane lands.
I saw such a face.
I saw the scars work

through the beauty
& repurpose it
into something

that could be smoked.

It Could Have Been a Picture

Every person in socks
& no shirt, we made grilled cheese
with hot dog buns

& American slices
& when each glorious orange
sandwich was laced

with peyote we all sat down
& rejoiced in the experience
of a world with such context.

We, each of us, had a dream
& we, each of us
used what we had to achieve it.

Jefferson Township, Ohio

The bees are here.
They're in our veins.
We are the hive,

because we have
mislabeled the honey.
We've tasted too little

& we've tasted too much
& since we cannot
trust the beekeepers,

we have the whole
countryside to ruin
with our stingers.

JELLOWAY, OHIO

A sigh
& you're through.

I Got Lost Every Time

We all missed
nowhere
& so I was trained

to forget everywhere
& I was trained
to fill light times

with darkness.
It changes,
but most drugs,

they work
almost every time.
It's beautiful.

Middlebury Township, Ohio

The all-
intention
wanes
& after
that we
are left

with abstract
reasons why
the whole
county
is using
the other

drugs.
We long
for the times
when Mount
Vernon
Republicans

sent drunks
from town
to town
to ensure
the county seat.
We know

what to do
with drunks.
These people
are eating
each other's
faces off.

KNOX COUNTY IS THE KETTLE

All fire
& water,
these people,

my people,
are still
refusing

to eat
red peppers
& not one

of them
has found
the tin

edges
of the problem.
This shrieking

isn't an alarm,
it's the throaty
piece,

the shuttle-
shake of death
declaring

this land
to be his
& not ours.

MONROE TOWNSHIP, OHIO

You can smoke anything.
Well, you can't smoke a bible.
That thin paper tears

& won't catch long enough.
You're better off eating your weed
in Monroe Township.

I Believe in the End of Forgiveness

Motherfuckers, you got high
& stole my kids' bikes
in the middle of the goddamn day.

HUNT, OHIO

A turn of the head
& we forget what
works through

our blood fast enough
to steal out heart's
behavior. Fuck teeth,

we need to he loved.
Fuck love, we need
to be filled up

by anything that
could be glory.
Fuck glory, fill me up.

I Won't Forget

The authentic
can be synthesized
& the degree

of the glowing
has never
mattered anyway.

It's a made
up world,
Right? Right?

Howard, Ohio

The rose abstracts
outside of the garden.
In the pizza shop

it could mean anything.
When it's stolen
from the pizza shop

it really only means
one thing. Love requires
more than meth

& four pizza pies.
It require care. It requires
that fucking rose.

QUICK ROOT

Some plunges are wings
melting into the good black dirt
& feeding that dirt

with the un-writing
of a person's book. Tongues
working past the failing bloom,

the drugs can subtract
you forever. They are taking
all of Ohio. It's a burial

of the living. It's the best
of us leeched to be lost
in the slight pull of gravity

& the claim each ounce
of each drug is making
on our once reminiscent flight.

Rich Hill, Ohio

Three shirts owned
& two of them buried
by the train tracks,

there is a boy holding
his last cloth wrapped
around his fists,

muscles developing
on the hood of his car
& I can't wait to hear

what he's going to say
to me. I can't wait
for the casual threat.

I've moved towards his car
just in case the Honda
has a bottom lip

I can step on.
This kid might be sober.
He's the only one

& that makes his
muscles matter more
to me than his *fuck you,*

old man. If he raises
his eyes from his phone
to hit me, there is hope.

PRELUDE

I didn't choose
to sleep
under the bed.

Pleasant Township, Ohio

The dogs
get fed last,
if they get fed

at all
& that is the fatal
flaw of anyone

taking more
drugs than
they're selling.

CHAIN-STORE IDENTITY

House of belonging,
cheap
& always discounted

by the land-owners,
I can always find myself
in your off-brand,

off-color revelries.
I've thrown parties
for the dead

with thirty pounds
of streamers
I bought for a dollar.

I've been found
without searching
in my worst of times

& I have never been
arrested for smoking
in your bathroom.

A mountain of sugar
for a quarter
& a safe place to get

high, I name
you my naming,
a church of sorts.

FREDERICKTOWN, OHIO

First church
of my first church,
the tomato

in my eye,
I blink to give
you the salt

you need. I cry,
because that red
curtain I saw

never swung open
& when the sun sets
I see no father

reaching down
to cradle
& halt your trade.

I trust the trucks
moving through
the grain lines.

I know what it means
when they drive
without lights on.

Danville, Ohio

Some nothings
are everything
& those moving

& robed communities
stay waist-deep
in the generations

& when one, two,
three, four, five
children die

like characters
in a newspaper story,
the crosswinds

give up completely.
The brownies cool
all on their own.

The football games
get louder
because they must.

You Can Do Anything in the Walmart as Long as You Don't Touch the Bicycles

House of my belonging,
I wore a dirty dress
& empty Coke twelve-packs

as shoes, I ate marshmallows
straight from the bag
& changed all of televisions

to a Thursday football game
& I definitely remember
peeing in a children's potty

& everything was rosy
until I unhooked one bike
& proved myself

to be an undeniable victor
in a short race that ended
near the bulk t-shirt aisle.

Monroe Mills, Ohio

The mercy
of the lord
is for the dead

& since we
hold so many
of our dead

without re-
membering
why they died,

the mercy
of the lord
is only

for the dead.
Nobody tosses
out the drugs

of the dead.
That's not how
this works.

Unless It's My Own

I have seen
Mount Vernon
poorly spent

& I have heard
no talk about
Mount Vernon

& I am told
about Fredericktown
& Danville

all of the time.
The whole county
is on fire

& we're arguing
about which
town uses

the least gasoline?
These drugs
are cheap

& they are magic
& it's all happening
somewhere else?

No. That heat
doesn't respond
to piss

& it's already caught
the bottom
of your pant leg.

UTICA, OHIO

There is a metaphysical assumption
that transcendence begins in the mind
& I have risen many times

that way, but in Central Ohio
it takes a little extra to be lifted
above the diamond cutters

& small-town politicians
that you know were forced
to leave the church deacons

because they were watching girls
change in the basketball locker room.
It takes good, hard drugs

to believe that you have the ability
to range into a naturalness
that feels as large as the world

& I find no fault in those that take
drugs to escape, but I miss
so many people

that never came back to me.

THE SEVENTEENTH HOUR

Somebody keeps buying tea.
I've never seen anybody drink tea
in a drug house.

Somebody keeps buying tea.
What self develops into a wolf
& howls for a cup of delicate leaf?

Somebody keeps buying tea
& it appears to be a firm decision,
that this house becomes a castle

made of tea bags. When the hot
water comes, will we all rise?
Somebody keeps buying tea.

North Liberty, Ohio

There! The enormous
sleeping woman
that is sitting on top

of the Kohler cooler
that is full of Pepsi Cola
& two thousand dollars

worth of cocaine.
There! A smile.
How lovely, her freckles

& sincere concern
that you know exactly
what it is we're doing here.

MOUNT VERNON, OHIO

The whole town,
my home town
is on the edge
of town
& even though
we've named
every stray township
they're still a part
of Mount Vernon
& even though
most of the fires
are outside
of city limits,
they all begin
in our parking lots
& in the few
apartments
around the circle.
Each long drive-
way is an opportunity.
Each trespassing sign
is an opportunity.
Every one of these drugs
passes our ball-fields.
Most of the dead cops
are ours. There is
lightning in our blood
& we are so tired
of being tired
of trying to keep up
with our own blood.
I've got teammates

dead from this shit.
So, right now
I'm forgetting how
lovely it was to grow
up around here.

Ode to the Corner of the Drug House Down the Gravel Road Off the Two-Lane Highway #1

Inhale the world.
The whole world
is in this wood-

paneling. I see it.
It's looking at me
with a fake eye,

a knot that is more
sigh than
any yellow moon.

Ode to the Corner of the Drug House Down the Gravel Road Off the Two-Lane Highway #2

Fingernails like lost blossoms,
I have carved all of my names
into what I cannot get back.

Ode to the Corner of the Drug House Down the Gravel Road Off the Two-Lane Highway #3

Homemade magic
is actual magic.
I love deeply

how simple
my life has become
with only corners

to contend with.
I roll my shoulders
& I am an epic.

ODE TO THE CORNER OF THE DRUG HOUSE DOWN THE GRAVEL ROAD OFF THE TWO-LANE HIGHWAY #7

The crumbling
is the mountain
climbing you.

ODE TO THE CORNER OF THE DRUG HOUSE DOWN THE GRAVEL ROAD OFF THE TWO-LANE HIGHWAY #8

So many little explosions
in the intimacy
of the intrusive craft

& now, there are more
people here to watch me
lose my common speech.

I've come back here
to stay lost here
& now the girl

my sister beat out
on the tennis team
shows up

with two packages
of corn tortillas?
Sure, I'll have one.

Ode to the Corner of the Drug House Down the Gravel Road Off the Two-Lane Highway #10

The fear is the cup.
The joy is in the river.
I'm in the plastic tub

in the middle
of the front lawn.
There's piss everywhere.

I can see forgiveness
is an ending that exists
outside of the elements.

Ode to the Corner of the Drug House Down the Gravel Road Off the Two-Lane Highway #13

The awful man
does awful things.
I know this

& yet, I cannot
flag the boxer
in my own heart.

I cannot ask
the crowd
why I'm here.

Ode to the Corner of the Drug House Down the Gravel Road Off the Two-Lane Highway #15

All smoke
from floor
to ground,

I fought
an enemy
the drugs

gave me.
That's how
drugs work

& while I
filled light
times

with dark-
ness, I lost
to conquest.

I fought dragons
that were on
the television.

ODE TO THE CORNER OF THE DRUG HOUSE DOWN THE GRAVEL ROAD OFF THE TWO-LANE HIGHWAY #18

These in-crowd alliances
are worthless. I don't even
get a discount on the wolf.

Ode to the Corner of the Drug House Down the Gravel Road Off the Two-Lane Highway #27

Some clouds
never pass.
Some clouds

grow roots
in your chest
& funnel

the rain
into the barrel
that once

held your id.
I slosh
with the nature

of my own
lost ego.
I'm nothing

being filled
up with some-
thing from

just south
of your
heavens.

ODE TO THE CORNER OF THE DRUG HOUSE DOWN THE GRAVEL ROAD OFF THE TWO-LANE HIGHWAY #29

Hardened in the air,
my mouth has gone
thin with the season,

which is no longer fall,
no longer winter,
this season is Ohio,

this season is the drug
season. The body
count is the same

as what it would take
to remove the context
of the stars in the sky.

ODE TO THE CORNER OF THE DRUG HOUSE DOWN THE GRAVEL ROAD OFF THE TWO-LANE HIGHWAY #33

The fence is made
of dirty carpets

& yet, rarely
does anyone escape.

Ode to the Corner of the Drug House Down the Gravel Road Off the Two-Lane Highway #38

Blue orange
& the empty
chicken nugget bags

we turned into bases
while the tobacco
pieces of our soul

stopped us from
running too fast
around the living

room, we played
one half of one
inning

& that is how
the television
got busted up.

Ode to the Corner of the Drug House Down the Gravel Road Off the Two-Lane Highway #41

Hat on a hat,
Tiki's virtual reality setup
lasted for an hour

before we tossed it
in the retention pond.
He'd driven to Columbus

& robbed three houses
before he could get that
at the Radio Shack

& then, the flat black
& gold coloring
freaked out

his brother a little
too much. I think
I prefer the simple

drugs working
through my simple
body,

but I felt bad he went
through all of that
to watch

a quick drowning
of a technology
we never understood.

Ode to the Corner of the Drug House Down the Gravel Road Off the Two-Lane Highway #44

From here,
the valley
looks like
a good fever.

Ode to the Corner of the Drug House Down the Gravel Road Off the Two-Lane Highway #48

How fantastic
the translation
of heroin

on a good
man's thoughts.
Light eaten

from the inside
& framed
so perfectly

that an actual
haunting
will occur.

Ode to the Corner of the Drug House Down the Gravel Road Off the Two-Lane Highway #49

Each moment tastes
like a foreign tongue
exploring my soul

& refusing to be
gentle as it refuses
to take me with it.

I can see the moon
from here. I can see
it turn away as well.

I have so many names
that nobody is willing
to say out loud anymore.

ODE TO THE CORNER OF THE DRUG HOUSE DOWN THE GRAVEL ROAD OFF THE TWO-LANE HIGHWAY #58

Bruises on top of bruises,
I can't get any more down
than I already am, officer.

Ode to the Corner of the Drug House Down the Gravel Road Off the Two-Lane Highway #59

Sure,
I'll eat the carpet.
There are a lot

of chips down here.
Fuck you.
I'm doing

what you told me
to do.
I don't know

how long the chips
have been down
here.

Ode to the Corner of the Drug House Down the Gravel Road Off the Two-Lane Highway #60

The eye of the haven
from the outside,
looks like a slit

an uneager wound
in a terrible house
& from the back

of this car I can feel
no prelude, I can see
no future. That

corner never knew
me sober.
I feel loss

will find me
once this shit
wears off

& then what will
I get to look out of?
I used to see all

of Ohio through
that damage.
I could smell

the water from
the retention pond
turning against me.

ACKNOWLEDGEMENTS

Cheat River Review – "Ode to the Corner #44"

GloryMag – "Unless It's My Own"

Gnarled Oak – "Ode to the Corner #51"

Minetta Review – "Ode to the Corner #60"

Misfit Magazine – "Jefferson Township, Ohio and Monroe Township, Ohio"

Pine Hills Review – "Sweet Wolf #1"

Rat's Ass Review – "Ode to the Corner #41"

RavensPerch – "Sweet Wolf #25"

Red Fez – "Fredericktown, Ohio"

Zombie Logic Review – "Sweet Wolf #12 and Sweet Wolf #13"

I owe many thank yous for the creation of this book. Thank you to Campbell McGrath for selecting it. Thank you to Trio House Press for the tremendous amount of love and enthusiasm they have shown my work. Thank you to the folks of Whetstone Library in Columbus, Ohio for always being so helpful when it's time for me to do research for a book like this. Thank you to my wife for allowing me the time to research, write, and pace over this book. This is not a topic that any Ohioan can handle lightly, and that weight was not lost on any of the people that either directly affected the writing of these poems or gave me the space to write them. I truly appreciate everyone that helped in even the smallest way. Thank you. Thank you. Thank you.

About the Author

Darren C. Demaree is from Mount Vernon, Ohio. He is a graduate of The College of Wooster and Miami University. He is the recipient of The Nancy Dew Taylor Prize from Emrys Journal, has received nine Pushcart Prize nominations, and has published six collections of poetry. Outside of his own poetry, Darren is the founding editor of *Ovenbird Poetry*, as well the Managing Editor of the Best of the Net Anthology. Currently, he is enrolled in Kent State University's M.L.I.S. program, and is living and writing in Columbus, Ohio, with his wife and children.

ABOUT THE ARTIST

Born in Jerusalem, Israel, **Michelle Frankfurter** is a
documentary photographer from Takoma Park, MD. She
graduated from Syracuse University with a bachelor's degree
in English. Before settling in the Washington, DC area,
Frankfurter spent three years living in Nicaragua where she
worked as a stringer for the British news agency, Reuters
and with the human rights organization Witness For Peace
documenting the effects of the contra war on civilians. In 1995,
a long-term project on Haiti earned her two World Press
Photo awards. Since 2000, Frankfurter has concentrated on
the border region between the United States and Mexico and
on themes of migration. She is a 2013 winner of the Aaron
Siskind Foundation grant, a 2011 Top 50 Critical Mass winner,
a finalist for the 2011 Aftermath Project and the 2012 Foto
Evidence Book Award for her project *Destino*, documenting
the journey of Central American migrants across Mexico. Her
first book, *Destino* was published in September 2014 by Foto
Evidence.

About the Book

Two Towns Over was designed at Trio House Press through the collaboration of:

Drew S. Cook, Lead Editor
Tayve Neese, Supporting Editor
Cover Photo: Michelle Frankfurter
Lea C. Deschenes, Interior & Cover Design

The text is set in Adobe Caslon Pro.

The publication of this book is made possible, whole or in part, by the generous support of the following individuals and/or agencies:

Anonymous

About the Press

Trio House Press is a collective press. Individuals within our organization come together and are motivated by the primary shared goal of publishing distinct American voices in poetry. All THP published poets must agree to serve as Collective Members of the Trio House Press for twenty-four months after publication in order to assist with the press and bring more Trio books into print. Award winners and published poets must serve on one of four committees: Production and Design, Distribution and Sales, Educational Development, or Fundraising and Marketing. Our Collective Members reside in cities from New York to San Francisco.

Trio House Press adheres to and supports all ethical standards and guidelines outlined by the CLMP.

The Editors of Trio House Press would like to thank Campbell McGrath.

CPSIA information can be obtained
at www.ICGtesting.com
Printed in the USA
FFOW02n1707010718
47244983-50098FF

9 780996 586498